THE CENCI

THE CENCI

a play by Antonin Artaud

translated by
Simon Watson Taylor

Grove Press, Inc., New York

Originally published in
Antonin Artaud, *Oeuvres Complètes,* Vol. IV
by Editions Gallimard 1964
© Editions Gallimard 1969

English translation
© 1969 SIMON WATSON TAYLOR

First Evergreen Edition, 1970

Library of Congress Catalog Card **Number:** 75-97158
Second Printing
Manufactured in the United States of America
DISTRIBUTED BY RANDOM HOUSE, INC., NEW YORK

Translator's Note

Antonin Artaud subtitled his play: *Tragédie en quatre actes, d'après Shelley et Stendhal*. Shelley wrote his five-act tragedy *The Cenci* in 1819, basing his version of the famous sixteenth-century story on the dossier of the affair in the Archives of the Palazzo Cenci in Rome. Stendhal translated this manuscript in 1837, published it in the *Revue des Deux Mondes*, and later incorporated it into his *Chroniques Italiennes*.

As far as the main characters are concerned, both Shelley and Artaud stick fairly closely to the facts, though the historical Monsignore Guerra has become transformed into the treacherous Orsino, and Cardinal Camillo is an invention of Shelley's which Artaud retains. The real-life murderer was the Castellan of Petrella: Shelley substitutes a pair of professional assassins, and Artaud in his turn makes them mutes.

Artaud follows Shelley's plot fairly closely for the first two acts and for the first scene of Act Three. His fourth act condenses Shelley's last two acts. In the first two acts of his version Artaud occasionally paraphrases Shelley, but most of the dialogue and all of the stage directions are entirely original. Indeed the *mise en scène* was far more important for Artaud than articulated language, which was to be used as a means of expressing the *mise en scène.* "It is not a question of suppressing spoken language,' wrote Artaud, "but of giving words the importance they have in dreams." The two articles by Artaud about *The Cenci,* published shortly before the play opened, which immediately follow this Note, provide an important insight into Artaud's intentions.

The present translation follows the text of the manuscript Artaud used for the staging of the play, including changes and additions penciled in during rehearsals.

There are two other extant manuscripts which contain a very great number of variants, and one of these includes whole scenes which were eliminated from the final version. For a complete list of these variants see Antonin Artaud, *Oeuvres Complètes,* edited by Paule Thévenin, Vol. IV, Gallimard, 1964, "Dossier des Cenci," pp. 325–339, and "Notes," pp. 389–417.

The Cenci

The Cenci, which will be performed at the Folies-Wagram from May 6 onwards, is not yet the Theater of Cruelty but is preparing the way for it.

I have drawn my play from Shelley and Stendhal, which does not mean that I have adapted Shelley or imitated Stendhal.

From both of them I have taken the subject, which is, in any case, historical and far more beautiful in nature than on the stage or in printed accounts.

Shelley added to nature his own style and that language of his which resembles a summer night bombarded by meteors, but personally I prefer nature in the raw.

In writing the tragedy *The Cenci* I have not sought to imitate Shelley any more than I have tried to copy nature, but I have imposed upon my tragedy the movements of nature, that kind of gravitation which moves the plants and moves human beings like plants, and which becomes concentrated in the form of the earth's volcanic eruptions.

The whole production of *The Cenci* is based on this gravitational movement.

The gestures and movements in this production are just as important as the dialogue; the purpose of the dialogue is to act as a reagent to the other elements. And I think it will be the first time, at least here in France, that a theatrical text has been written in terms of a production the modalities of which have sprung fully formed and alive from the author's imagination.

The difference between the Theater of Cruelty and *The Cenci* will be the difference which exists between the din of a waterfall or the unleashing by nature of a hurricane on the one hand and, on the other hand, whatever degree of their violence may remain in a recorded impression.

For example, it was impossible to make use of direct sound for *The Cenci:* in order to create a volume of vibration comparable to that of a cathedral's great bell I was obliged to record Amiens Cathedral's great bell with a microphone.

Just as they would in the Theater of Cruelty, the audience at *The Cenci* will find themselves in the center of a network of sound vibrations; but these, instead of emanating from four actual thirty-foot-high bells hanging at the four cardinal points of the auditorium, will be diffused by loudspeakers placed at these same points.

The Cenci will include the presence of human dummies, and in this way, again, I shall achieve the Theater of Cruelty by indirect and symbolic paths.

In *The Cenci* we will, in the first place, be listening to what the characters say; and they say more or less everything that they think; but we shall also find things that no one can say, however great may be his natural sincerity and the depths of his self-awareness. The dummies will be there to force the heroes of the play to describe the things that are troubling them and which human speech is incapable of expressing.

The dummies will be there to formulate all the reproaches, rancor, remorse, anguish, and demands, and the play will be filled from one end to the other with a whole language of gestures and signs in which the anxieties of the age will blend together in violent demonstration of feeling.

The Cenci is a tragedy in the sense that I am the first person for a very long time to have attempted to give speech not just to men but to *beings,* beings each of whom is the incarnation of great forces, while still retaining just enough human quality to make them plausible from the psychological point of view.

As though in a dream, we witness these beings roaring, spinning around, flaunting their instincts or their vices, passing like great storms in which a sort of majestic fate vibrates.

We have not yet reached the domain of the Gods, but we have almost reached the domain of the heroes such as they were conceived to be in Antiquity. In any case, the characters in *The Cenci* possess this exalted, legendary aspect, this atmosphere of rashness and bewilderment shining through the clouds which one finds in the heroes of those great stories and those marvelous epic poems.

It seems to me that *The Cenci* returns the theater to its true path and enables it to recapture that almost human dignity without which it can only waste the audience's time completely.

Antonin Artaud

(published in the review *La Bête Noire,* No. 2, May 1, 1935)

What the tragedy *The Cenci* at the Folies-Wagram will be about

In *The Cenci,* the father is destroyer, and in this way the theme may be assimilated to the Great Myths.

The tragedy *The Cenci* is also a Myth which spells out a few truths clearly.

And it is because *The Cenci* is a Myth that this theme has become a tragedy when transferred to the stage.

I say deliberately a tragedy rather than a drama; for here the men are more than men, even if they are not yet gods.

Neither innocent nor guilty, they are in the power of the same essential amorality which possessed those gods of the Mysteries of Antiquity from whom all tragedy has emanated.

What did the gods mean for the peoples of Antiquity?

Plato devotes page after page to discussing the nature of the gods.

What is certain is that these gods went straight on their way, oblivious of the pettifogging human distinctions between good and evil, almost as though they equated evil with betraying one's nature and good with remaining faithful to it, whatever the moral consequences. Indeed the gods never concerned themselves with moral consequences.

I have tried to imbue the characters in my tragedy with the same sort of fabulous amorality that belongs to lightning as it strikes, and to the boiling explosion of a tidal wave.

And I felt strongly that in an era such as ours, when nature speaks more loudly than man, it was appropriate to resuscitate an ancient Myth which pierces the heart of today's anxieties.

So much for the theme.

The next step was to make this Myth tangible, to endow it with speech: because even if nature does speak more loudly than man, I have the impression that, apart from a few very rare exceptions, the general tendency of the era has been to forget to wake up.

I have attempted to give a jolt to this hypnotic sleep by direct physical means. Which is why everything in my play turns, and why each character has his particular *cry*.

An important aspect of the production of this play will be an emphasis on symbolic gesticulation where a sign conveys the same significance as a written word.

That is to say that for me gesture is just as important as what is entitled language, because gesture is a language in its own right.

The lighting effects will also be treated with the importance due a language, and in this attempt to achieve a single, integrated theatrical language light will constantly be associated with sound in order to produce a total effect.

Balthus, the designer of the sets, is just as much at home with the symbolic nature of forms as he is conversant with that of colors; just as Desormière, whose musical inventions are a positive unleashing of the sounds of nature, is well aware of the communicative value of these sounds.

Gestures, sounds, noises, scenery, text, lighting: we have tried to offer the theater-going public of Paris a bold experiment which can compete today with those countries in Europe where the theater has once again become a religion.

Antonin Artaud

(published in *Le Figaro*
May 5, 1935)

THE CENCI

Characters

The Cenci was first performed at the Théâtre des Folies-Wagram, in Paris, on May 6, 1935, in a production directed by Antonin Artaud, with music by Roger Desormière and sets and costumes by Balthus. Artaud himself played the part of Count Cenci. Roger Blin was Artaud's production assistant, and played the first role of his acting career as one of the two mute Assassins.

ACT ONE

Scene One

A deep, winding gallery. CAMILLO *and* CENCI *enter, in conversation.*

CAMILLO: Pah! . . . A murder? That's nothing to get excited about! One body more or less is no great matter for those of us who have the cure of souls. Still, there are appearances to consider. Oh yes! Public morals, standards of conduct, a whole social façade which the Pope is determined to enforce. There you have the reason for his harshness toward you . . . and his rigorous demands. I had to exert every ounce of my influence at the conclave to persuade him to let you off. At a small price, of course. Give him your estate beyond the Pincian gate and he will erase your sins from his memory.

CENCI: A plague on it! the third of my possessions!

CAMILLO: You find that unreasonable?

CENCI: It is unreasonable that a man's life should be

valued at three measures of land with the vineyards that grow on them.

CAMILLO: Just what do you complain about?

CENCI: About my own cowardice.

CAMILLO: Perhaps you would rather have your crime publicly proclaimed?

CENCI: What then? Public knowledge of my crime does not mean that I shall suffer for it.

CAMILLO: What could you do?

CENCI: Fight! *That* I would really enjoy.—War on the papacy. This Pope is too greedy for riches. It has become too easy today for a man of power to bury his crimes under his piles of gold. I shall rally the common people against such arrogance. I tell you that I can and will beat back all the Pope's onslaughts from behind the fortifications of my castle in Petrella.

CAMILLO: Devil take it, man, what a fuss over a simple question of conscience!

CENCI: You know the difference between us? I don't torture my conscience as you do yours.

CAMILLO: Calm down, Count Cenci, calm down, please! I take it that you don't intend to stir up rebellion throughout the land to back up a crime which you have just been told has already been purged.

CENCI: That is the only thing that holds me back. A war would occupy my energies and keep me from doing something I have in mind!

CAMILLO: A new vileness, no doubt, a fresh horror in which your soul can wallow.

CENCI: Perhaps. That is my business. The Church has no authority to delve into my secret heart.

CAMILLO: Count Cenci, we are weary of battles. The world is exhausted and longs for peace. The Pope's gesture is a call to truce and appeasement.

CENCI: Ha! Then I shall celebrate this general amnesty with an orgy to which you shall all be invited. Yes, all you great chiefs of the nobility and the priesthood. A great orgy, as in pagan times, during which the vices of old Count Cenci will show you what peace really means.

CAMILLO: Enough, Count Cenci, enough! You almost make me regret my eloquence at the conclave. You are growing old, but you still have time to repent your past sins.

CENCI: Your Church jargon is sheer twaddle! The future and the past don't exist for me any longer, so the idea of repentance is meaningless. I have one aim left in life: to fashion more exquisitely refined crimes. And the one legacy I am determined to bequeath is a crowning glory of horror.

CAMILLO: Count Cenci, if I do not accuse you of childishness it is because I am paid to believe in your sincerity.

CENCI: At last! A man bold enough to understand me! Yes, I would indeed be a mere child if no one could bring himself to believe that I am truly a monster. You know very well that I am quite capable of carrying out any crime I imagine.

CAMILLO: It's not just the matter of a man's death that troubles me. After all, society, the hypocrite, has no qualms about sacrificing this precious human life. It does so willingly every time a *coup d'état,* a rebellion, a war gives it the excuse to hide behind the skirts of its habitual accomplice, destiny.

CENCI: You understand me well enough. Look at me! I am "old" Count Cenci, but tougher than my skinny frame may suggest. In my dreams I often find that I am destiny personified. Yes, *that* is the explanation of my vices: I tell you that the fountain of hatred welling up inside me is powerful enough to drown all my nearest kin. I feel—I know—that I am a force of nature. For me, life, death, god, incest, repentance, crime do not exist. I obey my own law. I can look into myself without becoming giddy, and so much the worse for anyone who trips and topples into the abyss which I have become. My destiny, my convictions order me to seek out evil, to practice evil. How can I resist the forces burning within me, bursting out of me?

CAMILLO: If I believed in God I would say that you were the living proof of the lessons taught by the ancient tales of the saints: you are more persuasive than Lucifer himself.

The voice of ANDREA *is heard in the corridor.*

ANDREA: My Lord, a man has arrived from Salamanca, claiming to have important and agreeable news to communicate to you.

CENCI: Excellent! Take him to the secret room. I will see him there.

CAMILLO: Goodbye. I shall still pray to the Lord that your impious and sacrilegious words may not tempt His spirit to abandon you utterly. (*Exit* CAMILLO.)

CENCI: The third of my possessions! And what is left is to serve to keep my children in pampered luxury? Ah God! Salamanca is not far enough away. Death is the only destination: we know by experience that those who visit *that* city are reluctant ever to show their faces again. Ah, how I hoped to be rid of those two. Funeral candles are my only future gift to them. The great difference between the villainies committed in real life and the villainies acted out on the stage is that in real life we do more and say less, while in the theater we talk endlessly and accomplish very little. Well, I shall restore the balance, and I shall restore it at the expense of real life. I shall lop some branches off my flourishing family. (*Here he starts counting on his fingers.*) Two sons down here, one wife here. As for my daughter, I shall lop her off too, but with a different implement! Evil must be allowed its portion of pleasure. I shall torture the soul by abusing the body: and when it is done as thoroughly as a living man can do it, then let anyone try to accuse me of being a mere play actor. Let anyone dare! (*Here, he holds out his hand straight and flat but with the little finger dangling.*) But there remains this thing that dangles: Bernardo. I shall leave them my young son Bernardo so that he may bemoan them. (*He blows out his breath.*) Air, I confide my thoughts to you. (*He paces up and down the gallery.*)

And you echoes of my steps, fly through the air. You are just as silent as my thoughts. Even the walls cannot hear you.

He draws his sword and strikes a violent blow on a gong. ANDREA, *the servant, appears.*

ANDREA: My Lord.

CENCI: Go to Beatrice, my daughter, tell her that I desire to see her alone. Tonight at midnight. Go.

Scene Two

Enter BEATRICE *and* ORSINO. *To the right, a gallery of the Cenci Palace. In the center, a moonlit garden.*

BEATRICE: Do you remember the spot where we first talked together? From here one can just see the cedar tree. The same moonlight as tonight bathed the slopes of the Pincio.

ORSINO: I remember: you said you loved me.

BEATRICE: You are a priest, do not speak to me of love.

ORSINO: What do my vows matter, now that I am with you again? No Church is powerful enough to battle with my heart.

BEATRICE: It is not the Church or your heart which keeps us apart, Orsino: it is fate.

ORSINO: What fate?

BEATRICE: My father—he is my unhappy fate.

ORSINO: Your father?

BEATRICE: Because of him, I am no longer made for human love. Only in death can love become real for me.

ORSINO: You must not think such dark thoughts. Whatever the obstacles, I know that I can vanquish them if only I may count on your support.

BEATRICE: My support? No, Orsino, do not count on it. It is too late. There is something more than a man pacing up and down within these vile walls and forcing me to remain here. There are two dear names which make my servitude bearable. The sufferings of Bernardo and my mother come before my thoughts of you, Orsino. For me, love no longer has the virtues of suffering. Duty is my only love.

ORSINO: I feel as though a strange wind is blowing. A wind heavy with dark mysteries. Come to confession: the Blessed Sacrament will exorcise these wild fantasies.

BEATRICE: No Sacrament can conquer the cruelty that has me in its grips. Only action. Orsino: tonight my father is giving a great banquet. He has heard some happy news from Salamanca about my brothers there but this outward show of love is simply a mask for his inward hate. The impudent hypocrite! He would take more real joy in celebrating their deaths. Yes, I have seen him on his knees, praying aloud for just that. Oh God, that such a man should be my father! Great preparations have been made. All our kin, the Cenci, will be there, and all the chief nobility of Rome. He has sent orders to my mother and myself to wear our finest robes. Poor lady! she expects some happy change in his dark spirit from all this: I know differently. During supper, we will talk again about my love. Now I must leave you. (*Exit* BEATRICE.)

ORSINO: During supper! I shall not wait until then. I need your love, Beatrice, and I would be a fool to let you escape me. (*Exit* ORSINO).

Scene Three

CENCI, CAMILLO, BEATRICE, LUCRETIA, GUESTS *including* PRINCE COLONNA: *a number of dummy figures. The scene resembles that depicted in Veronese's* The Marriage of Cana, *but is far more savage in atmosphere. Purple curtains flap in the breeze, falling back against the wall in heavy folds. Then suddenly, framed by a draped curtain, a scene of orgy, looking like a painting done in trompe l'oeil, breaks into violent action. The bells of Rome can be heard in full peal, but muffled, following the dizzy rhythm of the banquet. Voices are raised, taking on the deep or high-pitched, almost crystal-clear note of the bells. From time to time, a thick heavy sound spreads out then dissolves, as though stopped by some obstacle which makes it rebound in sharp ridges.*

CENCI (*rises, already slightly the worse for drink*): My dear friends, solitude is a bad counselor. I have lived like a hermit for too long. Some of you, I know, have thought me dead—have, I would venture to say, even rejoiced in my death, without, however, daring to replace me by my own descendants. I have myself taken advantage of this general malevolence by indulging myself in the occasional pleasure of contemplating the Myth which I have become. I have sum-

moned you all today to tell you that the Cenci Myth
has come to an end, and that I am ready to make my
legend real. Feel these bones and tell me if they are
made to endure a life of silence and meditation.

CAMILLO: Is there a draft in the room? A strange current
of cold air has just sent a shiver down my spine.

A GUEST: These preliminary remarks sound ominous.

ANOTHER GUEST (*in a stifled voice*): If I remember cor-
rectly, Count Cenci, you invited us here to help you
celebrate some important event.

CENCI: I have invited you all here to confirm a legend, not
to destroy one. But first, I ask you this question:
have I, in fact, committed the crimes imputed to me?
You, Prince Colonna, you reply.

PRINCE COLONNA *rises.*

COLONNA: I believe I understand you. Looking at you, I
shall say simply that all of us here, such as we are, are
equally capable of committing murder.

CENCI: That is precisely what I intended you to say: none
of us has the face of a murderer.

Here each GUEST *glances stealthily at his neighbor.*

CAMILLO: I understand you dimly. Your way of speaking
is not very Catholic; but my acquaintance with the
language of the Church allows me to divine your
meaning. Yet I would hesitate to guess what new vil-
lainy may emerge from this occasion.

A GUEST: We thought that some holy purpose had inspired
you to call us together here.

CENCI: What purpose more holy than the one which fills my paternal heart with joy, and shows me that God has answered my prayers abundantly?

A GUEST: Answered your prayers! What prayers?

BEATRICE (*seated, is by now extremely agitated and makes as if to rise*) : My God! I think I know what he is going to say.

LUCRETIA (*placing a hand on her shoulder*) : No, no, calm yourself, dearest child.

CENCI: I have two sons who have never ceased tormenting my paternal heart. It is on their account that my prayer has been answered.

BEATRICE (*speaking positively and prophetically*) : Something frightful has happened to my brothers.

LUCRETIA: Ah no, he would not speak in that cynical tone!

BEATRICE: I am frightened.

CENCI: Here, Beatrice, read these letters to your mother. And let anyone say after this that the heavens are not on my side.

BEATRICE *hesitates.*

Here, take them, read what I have done for your brothers. (*Old Count Cenci's aggressive glance slowly ranges the hall.*) So, you refuse to understand: my disobedient and rebellious sons are dead. Dead, destroyed, finished, do you hear? Oh, speak, by all means, if you wish, of paternal solicitude: two bodies less to trouble me.

LUCRETIA, *who has also risen, falls heavily into Beatrice's arms.*

BEATRICE: It is not true. Open your eyes, dear Mother. The heavens would already have split in two if it were not a lie. No one can defy God's justice with impunity.

CENCI: May God's thunderbolt strike me down if I am lying. You will soon see that this justice which you invoke is on my side. (*He brandishes the letters above his head.*) The first has died beneath the rubble of a church vault which collapsed and buried him. The second was stabbed in error by a jealous man, while the woman they both loved was making love with their rival. Let anyone tell me now that Providence is not on my side.

A GUEST: Torches, torches, torches: torches to light my way; I am leaving!

CENCI: Wait.

ANOTHER GUEST: Yes, stay. He must be joking. A loathsome joke, indeed, but it must be a joke.

CENCI (*raising a goblet of wine*) : This wine is not a joke. The priest drinks his God at Mass. Who then can prevent me from believing that I am drinking the blood of my sons?

THE SAME GUEST: You are not even mad, you are simply grotesque. Come, let us all leave.

CAMILLO: Cenci, you are not in your right mind. I still wish to believe that you are dreaming. Let me tell them that you are unwell.

A GUEST: Yes, yes. I must be dreaming that I have heard all this.

Noise and confusion. The GUESTS *rush toward the exit.*

CENCI: I drink to the perdition of my family. If there is a God, may the heartfelt curses of a father tear them all from the throne of God.

A great silence descends. The scene of wild confusion is transformed into a tableau. Everyone stands frozen still.

Here, Andrea, pass round the goblet.

ANDREA, *trembling, approaches a group of* GUESTS. *One* GUEST *sends the goblet flying with a stroke from the back of his hand the moment it is proffered to him.*

THE GUEST (*in a voice stuttering with rage*): Assassin! Is there no man here who will help me cram these blasphemous words down his throat?

CENCI: To your seats, or not one man leaves this room alive.

The GUESTS *surge back from all sides in disorder. Panic-stricken, their tread is uncertain, and they move as though going into battle, but a battle of ghosts. They are off to fight ghosts, arms outstretched as though their hands were clutching a lance or a shield.*

BEATRICE (*barring the exit to them*): For pity's sake, do not go, noble guests. You are fathers. Do not leave us with this savage beast, or I shall never be able to look at the white hairs of an old man without feeling the desire to blaspheme fatherhood.

CENCI (*addressing the* GUESTS, *who are huddled in one corner*) : She speaks the truth; you are all fathers. Which is why I advise you to think about your off-spring before saying a single word about what has just happened here.

BEATRICE circles the stage at a run, ending up standing squarely in front of her father.

BEATRICE: You, take care.

CENCI lifts his hand as if to strike her.

Take care, lest God, receiving the curse of an evil father, should give weapons to his sons.

Here, the whole crowd, as if it had received a powerful punch in the stomach, draws in its breath, and exhales it in a great cry; BEATRICE *circles the stage again, ending up facing the crowd this time.*

Cowards! Have you not yet chosen between him and us?

CENCI: Go on. Join together to strike me down. Your united forces will not be enough. Now get out, all of you; I wish to be alone with her.

He points at BEATRICE. *The* GUESTS *retreat in a mass, in a general scurry; only* COLONNA *and* CAMILLO *make any attempt to face up to him, and they leave together in a dignified manner.* BEATRICE, *who has been looking after* LUCRETIA, *seems not to have heard Cenci's last words. She is on the point of following the others.* LUCRETIA, *who has regained consciousness, begins to sob.*

LUCRETIA: My God! What has he said now?

CENCI (*to* LUCRETIA) : You, go to your room. (*To* BEATRICE, *advancing toward her.*) You, not so fast. You will not leave before you have heard me out fully.

LUCRETIA *makes a gesture to* CENCI *of barring his way.* BEATRICE *shakes her head slightly to dissuade her.* LUCRETIA *understands and withdraws gently after one last glance at* BEATRICE. BEATRICE *and old* CENCI *remain face to face. They stare at each other steadily for a long moment.* CENCI *goes to the table and pours himself a fresh glass of wine. Several torches flicker out suddenly. The bells can be heard; their tone has become sepulchral. An extraordinary calm descends upon the scene. Something like the sound of a viola vibrates very lightly and very high up.* BEATRICE *sits down in a chair and waits.* CENCI *approaches her gently. His attitude is completely transformed; it radiates a sort of serene emotion.* BEATRICE *looks at him and it seems that her own misgivings too have suddenly vanished.*

(*In a humble tone touched with deep emotion.*) Beatrice.

BEATRICE: Father. (*She speaks the words that follow in a deep voice filled with emotion.*) Withdraw from me, impious man. I shall never forget that you were my father, but withdraw. On this condition I might perhaps be able to forgive you.

CENCI (*passes his hand across his forehead*) : Your father is thirsty, Beatrice. Will you not give your father a drink?

BEATRICE *goes to the table and brings him back a great goblet filled with wine.* CENCI *takes the goblet and makes a tentative gesture of passing his hand over Beatrice's hair.* BEATRICE, *whose head was bent slightly forward, suddenly jerks it back violently.*

(*In a low voice, between clenched teeth.*) Ah! viper, I know a charm that will make you meek and tame.

Hearing these last words of Cenci's, BEATRICE *feels herself filled with utter panic. As he finishes the sentence she darts away as though she has understood fully.* ANDREA, *who is following his master's movements, makes the gesture of barring the way to* BEATRICE.

Let her go.

A pause.

Let her go; the charm is working. Now she cannot escape me.

ACT TWO

Scene One

A room in the Cenci Palace, containing a great bed in the center. Dusk is about to fall. BERNARDO *and* LUCRETIA *are in the room.*

LUCRETIA (*rocking* BERNARDO *in her arms*) : Do not cry. I am not your true mother, but I love you just as though I were. Ah, how I have suffered. You know, Bernardo, for a sensitive woman each great mental suffering is like giving birth to a child.

BEATRICE *bursts in, panic-stricken.*

BEATRICE: Has he passed this way? Have you seen him, Mother? (*She listens attentively.*) There! I hear his step on the staircase. Is that not his hand at the door? Since yesterday, I feel his presence everywhere. I am exhausted, Lucretia. Help us, Mother, help us. I cannot go on fighting much longer.

LUCRETIA *takes Beatrice's head between her hands. Silence. Outside, the shrill cry of birds. Very high overhead, there is a sound like a footstep.*

Oh! this footstep which the walls echo. His footstep.
I see him as if he were there: his dreadful face lights
up. I should hate him and yet I cannot. His living
image is within me like the conscience of a crime.

LUCRETIA: Peace, peace, my child. A crime only exists
when it is committed.

BEATRICE *wrings her hands, and suddenly a sob is
wrenched from her, a sound which becomes a loud
wail.*

BEATRICE: I would rather die than give in to him.

LUCRETIA: Give in to him?

BEATRICE: Yes. Can you imagine a father bold enough to
dare allow such a monstrous scheme to ripen and grow
within himself, to nourish it without his courage
failing him?

LUCRETIA: But tell me, what can he have dared to do?

BEATRICE: Is there anything he dares not do? Everything
I have endured so far is nothing compared with what
he is preparing to do to me. He has made me eat foul,
rotting food. Day after day he has forced me to witness my brother's slow martyrdom, and you know
that I have never protested. But now . . . now . . .

*She wrings her hands and sobs bitterly. The door
opens.* BEATRICE *gives a violent start and leaps to her
feet, standing rigidly tense: the* LADY'S MAID *appears.*
BEATRICE *sits down again, her fears quieted.*

Thank you, dear God, it is not my father.

MAID: Monsignor Orsino begs to know at what hour he
might see you in strict privacy.

LUCRETIA: This evening, at the church.

The MAID *leaves the room, and suddenly the footsteps heard at the beginning of the scene grow increasingly loud.* BEATRICE, *who is listening intently, gets up once again.* CENCI *enters the room.*

BEATRICE: Ah!

CENCI, *who was moving in the direction of* BERNARDO, *suddenly sees* BEATRICE.

CENCI: Ah!

Then, as though he were preparing to take a grave decision, he utters a further "ah!"

Ah!

BEATRICE, *in a corner, trembles like a doe and makes an involuntary movement as though preparing to dash from the room, but without bringing herself to do it.*

(*Advancing toward her.*) You will stay, Beatrice. Last night, you dared to look me in the face.

BEATRICE, *who is trembling more and more, starts to collapse, sliding down the wall.*

(*Seizing her by the arm.*) Well! What are you waiting for?

LUCRETIA (*stepping between them*) : No, I beg you!

CENCI: You have probed me too deeply for me to feel shame any longer for what I am thinking.

LUCRETIA: I beg you, dear husband, have mercy, she is fainting. Do not torture her.

BERNARDO, *who has got up, comes up behind* LUCRETIA.

CENCI: Get away, old woman.

(*To* BERNARDO.) And you too: the sight of you reminds me of certain nasty love affairs which ruined the years of my manhood. Go, I loathe womanish creatures. Away with him. His milksop face makes me want to vomit.

LUCRETIA *gestures to* BERNARDO *to withdraw.* BERNARDO *starts toward the door, then, suddenly, dashes over to* BEATRICE, *seizes her by the hand and tries to drag her with him.*

Stop . . . On second thought, no. I always know where I can find the one of you two who interests me.

BEATRICE *and* BERNARDO *exit.* CENCI, *after pacing the room for a few moments, stretches out comfortably on the bed.*

LUCRETIA: Are you in pain?

CENCI: Yes. My family: that is my wound.

LUCRETIA (*in a tone of deep commiseration*): Alas! each new word you utter strikes us like a blow.

CENCI (*sitting on the edge of the bed*): What of it! It is my family that has corrupted everything.

LUCRETIA: What of it? Why, it is your very family which has allowed you to show the full measure of your cruelty! Without your family, what would you be?

CENCI: A human relationship between creatures born only to jostle for supremacy, creatures burning to devour each other? Impossible!

LUCRETIA: My God!

CENCI: Devil take your God.

LUCRETIA: But with such words no society can survive.

CENCI: The family which I have created and which I command is my sole society.

LUCRETIA: That is tyranny.

CENCI: Tyranny is my one last weapon to frustrate the war you are plotting against me.

LUCRETIA: There is no war, Cenci, except the war raging inside your head.

CENCI: There is the war you are waging against me and which I am more than capable of returning in kind. Do you dare to deny that you persuaded my daughter to turn last night's banquet into a meeting of murderers?

LUCRETIA: In the name of God, I have never harbored such thoughts.

CENCI: Not content with murder, you make use of criminal slander. In your fear of what my piercing mind might detect, you have done your best to get me locked up as a madman. You, my daughter Beatrice, and my sons, of whom the Providence which you invoke has just rid me, all of you were part of the vile plot.

LUCRETIA: I am suffocating.

CENCI: Blame yourself for the atmosphere you inhale.

LUCRETIA: Allow me to withdraw to some place where I may tremble in peace.

CENCI: You may indeed prepare to tremble, but not in the way you imagine. You, Beatrice, and that abortion whom you cluck over as though you had brought him into the world, all of you get ready to pack your things.

LUCRETIA (*with a sigh of resignation*): Where are we going?

CENCI: To Petrella. My estates contain a silent fortress which has never betrayed a breath of any secret confided to it. There you can plot in peace.

LUCRETIA: If I were you, I would pause for breath before continuing such accusations.

CENCI: Breathe, in this pestilential atmosphere!

LUCRETIA: Your sacrilegious imagination alone has created the atmosphere which makes you suffer.

CENCI: If I suffer, then I alone can deliver myself from my suffering. For the present, I place you in solitary confinement.

Exit LUCRETIA. *Night falls in the high-ceilinged room.* CENCI *moves slowly toward a part of it on which light is still falling.*

(*Taking a few steps near the door through which* LUCRETIA *has just left.*) And you, night, you who magnify everything, enter here (*striking himself on the chest*) with the vast shapes of all the crimes imaginable. You cannot expel me from myself. The act I carry within me is greater than you.

Scene Two

An indeterminate place. Heath, passageway, flight of steps, arcade, or any other setting. Shadows lie thick over everything. Enter CAMILLO *and* GIACOMO.

CAMILLO: Yes, yes, I know only too well that you are a Cenci. But if I have any advice to give you it is this: stop plaguing the Pope with your demented petitions.

GIACOMO: What do you mean, Signor Camillo?

CAMILLO: I mean that you share all the faults of the Cenci family but lack their essential toughness. If your father has robbed you of your inheritance, have it out with him; don't try to wheedle the Pope's help in your sordid quarrels.

GIACOMO: So I must do battle, must I? I must seize my own father by the scruff of his neck?

CAMILLO: Yes, if you have the courage, which I doubt. Of all the Cencis, you are the only one capable of trembling at the idea of a murder.

GIACOMO: But what you are asking me to do is to declare war not only against my father but against authority.

CAMILLO: A dangerous course of action to propose, perhaps, but I must admit that it gives me no cause for heart-searching. There was a time once when sons held their old parents in servitude, but with this devil of a Cenci we are in an age where the fathers' narrow despotism provokes their sons into rebellion.

GIACOMO: For a priest of Jesus Christ you speak a very strange language. I doubt whether the anarchy you recommend is so very desirable. Your Pope is like the sleeping man in the fable: each time he tosses and turns in his dreams, his priests translate his dream into action and provoke us into killing each other. Be careful! If I do as you suggest, my actions might turn into a kind of war against your own authority.

Between each of their words, their feet move as though they were still walking, but in fact the distance they travel in one direction or another is far less than would normally be the case.

CAMILLO: An armed uprising would by no means displease me if I were persuaded of its limited nature.

GIACOMO: Is it not on your advice, you treacherous snake, that the Pope has suggested to my father that he attempt to disinherit us?

CAMILLO: Our exalted monarchy of the Church is no less assiduous than the temporal monarchy in its hatred of feudalism.

GIACOMO: So?

CAMILLO: Do you not understand that old Cenci's fortune, his treasures, castles, and estates must inevitably revert to the papacy over the heads of his family?

GIACOMO: Your cynicism would disgust the faithful, if indeed the Catholic Church still harbors any such.

CAMILLO: I have never feared to argue in full conclave

everything which I have just said. Popes are created by the exercise of cynicism.

A pause. They can be heard starting to walk up and down again. But their bodies hardly move.

GIACOMO: If it was only poverty that afflicted me, I would not hesitate to leave for good. But I am utterly revolted by this country where the old people hold the whip hand. A man can always make a new life for himself if he has the support of his kinsmen. But I can no longer count on my own family. By robbing me of my honor, my father has hoped to rob me of their love.

CAMILLO: How so?

GIACOMO: He has made me a cuckold, a laughingstock. Yes, that is what I am in the eyes of my own wife. She feels nothing but contempt for me, and her sons hover about her life like unspoken reproaches.

CAMILLO: Ah, now I understand perfectly.

GIACOMO: Yes, contempt and the hatred it gives rise to are the sole legacy Cenci has left me.

CAMILLO: Listen. No one must have the least inkling of what I am about to propose to you.

GIACOMO: Ah! speak quickly.

Here, a hurried step can be heard. CAMILLO *backs away and disappears. Enter* ORSINO.

CAMILLO (*in a breathy whisper*) : Ah, here comes someone who can give you better advice than I could.

ORSINO: What have you been plotting with that spoiled priest?

GIACOMO: I? Nothing. You know the trouble I am in. This priest thinks you might have a plan which could solve my problems.

ORSINO: You, your brothers, your sister, your father— none of you will rest content until you have created havoc. (*Aside.*) My one desire is to give this wretched family the means to destroy each other. . . As you know, I should have married Beatrice. But the old man's crazy antics made me finally abandon such hopes. A strange fate seems to have descended on your whole family: the sons die, the father is mentally unbalanced, the daughter broods in an intolerable mysticism. I know you were not in Rome last night, but you must have heard rumors of the scandal which broke out in the home from which you are forever barred—Cenci's Palace.

GIACOMO: What scandal?

ORSINO: He locked all the doors and the guests feared their last hour had come. I only found out about it myself through the gossip of the scullions. None of the guests dare open their mouths.

GIACOMO: Can it be so?

ORSINO: Come now! Surely you have not forgotten the tainted blood stirring in your veins? The fact remains: old Cenci has succeeded in silencing his guests.

GIACOMO: He cannot get away with such blackmail. Not

in this day and age! We are living in the sixteenth century, in an age of progress.

ORSINO: Nevertheless, your sister and Lucretia have been reduced to a state of absolute terror.

GIACOMO: Hmm . . . that is not altogether unwelcome news. After all, I too am a victim of his tyranny.

ORSINO: Something tells me, Signor Cenci, that this tyranny cannot last much longer. I spoke with the Pope recently to try to stir his interest in the sufferings of your terrorized family. His Holiness laughed in my face. He asked me rhetorically: "Am I to set myself up against the natural authority of a father? Am I to enfeeble in this manner the principle of my own authority?" Then he answered himself: "No, never." You must rely upon yourself. When justice flies out of the window, the victims of oppression do well to show solidarity and defy the law.

GIACOMO: I am desperate enough to consider any scheme. In any case, I no longer have anything to lose.

ORSINO: The world is trembling on the edge of a precipice. This is the moment to try anything. I leave you, Signor Giacomo. Think about what I have just said. And remember that the interests of your family are from now on united with those of my own.

ACT THREE

Scene One

LUCRETIA *is alone as the curtain rises.* BEATRICE *bursts onto the stage, as if demented.*

BEATRICE: Armor, a fortified castle! . . . An army . . . A secret breastplate . . . Anything to keep him away from me . . .

LUCRETIA: Who?

BEATRICE: My father!

LUCRETIA: What has he done? . . . I hardly dare understand you!

BEATRICE: But you must understand. The worst has happened.

LUCRETIA: The worst? What new torment can he possibly have imagined?

BEATRICE: Cenci, my father, has defiled me.

She bursts into sobs. LUCRETIA *crosses the stage, making the sign of the cross four times.*

LUCRETIA: My God! My God! My God! My God!

BEATRICE (*between sobs*) : All is tainted. All. My body has been made a filthy thing, but it is my soul that has become truly polluted. There is no longer a single fragment of myself in which I can take refuge.

LUCRETIA *stands near her.*

LUCRETIA: Tell me what happened.

BEATRICE *sobs four times, between sighs.*

BEATRICE: My one crime is to have been born. I can choose my death, but I didn't choose my birth. *That* is the stroke of fate.

She embraces Lucretia's knees, like Mary Magdalen at the foot of the cross.

Tell me, mother, are all families alike? Then I could absolve myself of the injustice of being born.

LUCRETIA (*withdrawing slightly*) : Hush, you almost make me condemn the justice which allows such abominable crimes.

BEATRICE: Now I know how lunatics suffer. Madness is like death. I am dead, and yet my soul clings desperately to life and cannot free itself from its bonds.

LUCRETIA (*kneeling in front of her*) : I beg you, Beatrice, do suffer: I will try to comfort you. But return to your senses. When you rave like this, I too am lost. I beg you, return to your senses, or I shall believe that we are all possessed.

BEATRICE: You mothers know only how to grieve. And

yet, here, beneath our feet, are massing the forces of a world getting ready to sweep us all away.

LUCRETIA (*hiding her head in her hands*): My God! I have a terrible fear that the worst has not yet happened.

BEATRICE (*between sobs*): This savage world has witnessed horrible things, monstrous couplings, strange confusions of good and evil. But imagination never dreamed . . .

A pause.

When I was small, there was a dream which I dreamed every night. I am naked in a large room and a wild animal, the kind that appears in dreams, is breathing heavily . . . I realize that my body is shining.—I want to escape, but first I must hide my blinding nakedness . . . At that moment a door opens . . . I am hungry and thirsty and, suddenly, I discover that I am not alone . . . No! . . . There is not only the animal breathing beside me, it seems that there are other creatures breathing; and soon I see a mass of vile things swarming at my feet . . . And this multitude, too, is famished . . . I set out stubbornly, determined to try to find the light once more; for I feel that only the light will allow me to eat and drink my fill . . . But the animal is still close behind me, chasing me through cellar after cellar. Then I feel it upon me and realize that my hunger is not merely willful. And, each time, just as my strength ebbs away I awake very suddenly . . . Lucretia, you have been so like a mother to me! Today, my dream seems strangely distant.

LUCRETIA: Your dream simply says what I already know: that no one can escape his fate.

BEATRICE: If only I could believe what I have dreamed, that my childhood dream has overtaken me, and that a door on which a knock will soon be heard will open and will tell me once again that it is time for me to wake from sleep.

Someone knocks very gently on the door. The door opens almost immediately. ORSINO *enters, followed by* GIACOMO, *who hides behind him.*

Orsino, tell me: is it really a family law that fathers must rid themselves of their sons before possessing their daughters?

ORSINO: What can she mean?

BEATRICE: I mean that Cenci, my father, has just committed the most monstrous of all his crimes.

ORSINO: It is in his nature to . . . No, it cannot be.

BEATRICE: Do not trouble to ask yourself whether it can be or cannot be. It is, and it has been. And now, advise me how I can make sure it shall not be again.

LUCRETIA: Orsino, if you can do anything for us, intervene, I implore you; I am frightened.

ORSINO: There are judges. Draw up a complaint. Surrender your father to the secular arm.

BEATRICE: What judge can give me back my soul? Orsino, there is blood running in my veins which should not be there. From now on I can believe only in the justice which I myself shall choose.

ORSINO: What justice?

BEATRICE: I do not know . . . but something must be done! Something immense which will erase the very shadow of this crime. I have thought of killing myself, but I fear that even death will not give me refuge from an unexpiated crime.

ORSINO: Killing yourself? Do not juggle with images; that sort of justice is for madmen.

BEATRICE: Suggest something, then. Speak! I would lend myself to any measure, however atrocious. It is vital that we act without delay.

ORSINO: I favor an effective justice which achieves what it has set out to do. I am by no means against the idea of violence, but it must be a profitable violence. I detest the kind of flamboyant act which is invariably botched. Now then! You want to be revenged? And above all you want to prevent Cenci from repeating his vileness?

BEATRICE: Yes.

ORSINO: Then don't stir up public opinion. Act. But act discreetly. This is a case for secret assassins.

BEATRICE: Why secret? I would gladly stand in the public squares and cry out that my father has dishonored me.

ORSINO *beckons.* GIACOMO *appears and takes a step forward.*

ORSINO: I bring you another unfortunate. Advise *him* to cry through the town that Cenci, his father, has robbed him of his inheritance. My own justice is prudent and knows how to choose the means guaranteed to prevent failure. (*He beckons them all into a corner.*) Take Giacomo with you. Act in a body. Put Bernardo in the secret. Unite against this warped authority. Rebuild a family. The most successful conspirators are those bound by ties of family blood. With Bernardo you will be four. Remain four in the secret of the act. As for the act itself, I have two mutes . . .

BEATRICE: !!!!!!!!!!

LUCRETIA: !!!!!!!!!!

ORSINO: Yes, two brutish, dull-witted scoundrels who would kill a man as unthinkingly as we might tear a piece of paper in two. Such scum are plentiful nowadays, but this couple have one advantage over ordinary assassins: their mouths are sealed by nature.

BEATRICE: Even so we must be quick, Orsino. Tomorrow morning will already be too late.

LUCRETIA: Do you know that loathsome, savage fortress called Petrella? He means to incarcerate us there.

BEATRICE: He must not succeed.

ORSINO: Will it still be daylight when you get there?

LUCRETIA: The sun will only just have set.

BEATRICE: But I remember that two miles from the castle the path comes to a kind of chasm—deep down, a black torrent of water frothing and eddying ceaselessly through rocky caverns—and at that point a bridge spans the chasm.

Here, the sound of a footstep can be heard.

LUCRETIA: Dear God! It must be Cenci, unexpectedly returned.

BEATRICE: That step we hear approach must never pass the bridge.

They all withdraw.

GIACOMO (*as he leaves*): Family, gold, justice: I despise them all.

Scene Two

Dusk. The scene follows the last one without interruption. A fearful storm breaks out. Several claps of thunder explode at close intervals. Immediately, ORSINO *can be seen entering, followed by his two* ASSASSINS. *They are struggling against a violent wind.* ORSINO *posts his* ASSASSINS.

ORSINO: Yes, you understand well enough. We ourselves are the hurricane, so scream your lungs out if you wish.

GIACOMO: Do you think they know how to go about it? Just tell them to strike their man down, don't confuse them by telling them to match their silent throats with the screech of the hurricane.

Three thunderclaps reverberate. Several armor-clad men appear, moving extraordinarily slowly, like the figures on the face of the great clock of Strasbourg Cathedral. Repeated peals of thunder.

ORSINO: Calm yourself. Everything is all right. Each of the two knows the part he has to play.

GIACOMO: My fear is that they may overplay their parts and be no longer capable of doing anything real.

The jerky tramping of feet can be heard again. LUCRETIA, BERNARDO, BEATRICE *appear, walking at the same snail-like pace, and very far behind them, bringing up the rear, is* COUNT CENCI. *The storm rages with increasing fury, and, mingled with the wind, one can hear voices repeating the name Cenci, first in a single prolonged, high-pitched tone, then like the pendulum of a clock:*

CENCI, CENCI, CENCI, CENCI.

At moments all the names blend together at one point in the sky, like countless birds whose individual flights have converged together. Then the voices grow louder and pass by, like a flight of birds very close at hand.

CENCI (*facing the voices, shouts into the storm*): WHAT, THEN!

Immediately, the outlines of the ASSASSINS *can be seen surging forth, spinning like tops and meeting and passing each other in the illumination of a flash of lightning. At the same time, the roar of two pistol shots is heard. Night has fallen, the lightning flashes cease. Everything vanishes.*

GIACOMO: What, failed?

ORSINO: FAILED!

ACT FOUR

Scene One

CENCI *enters, pushing* LUCRETIA *in front of him.*

CENCI: Where is she hiding, eh? Where is she hiding? Desire, fury, love, I do not know . . . but I burn. I hunger for her . . . Go find her for me.

LUCRETIA: Enough . . . enough . . . enough . . . I need air. A moment of quiet. I want to live. We were not born to be tortured.

CENCI: And I, can you tell me why I was born?

LUCRETIA: I do not know why you were born, but I know that the sheer weight of your crimes has turned your life into something perilous, Cenci, something very perilous and vulnerable.

CENCI: Tut! Go find her for me.

LUCRETIA *exits. Suddenly* CENCI *staggers, and passes his hand across his forehead.*

(*With a forced laugh.*) I, repent! Why? Repentance

is in the hands of God. It is for Him to regret my act. Why has He created me father of a being whom I desire utterly? Let those who condemn my crime first indict fate. Free? Who dares still talk of freedom when the very sky is ready to fall? (*He moves downstage.*) That is why I open the floodgates. So that I shall not drown. I harbor a demon whose task is to avenge the whole world's sins. Now no fate can stop me from carrying out everything I have dreamed.

CENCI *disappears.* BEATRICE *enters with the* ASSASSINS. *There is rather a long pause. The sound of a footstep can be heard faintly.* BEATRICE *thrusts the two* ASSASSINS *into a corner.* LUCRETIA *appears.*

BEATRICE: Do you think he is asleep?

LUCRETIA: I put a sleeping potion in the wine he drank before retiring. But only a moment ago I heard him still crying out.

BEATRICE *beckons to the* ASSASSINS *to come forward.*

BEATRICE: I hope that this time you will dispatch things better than you did last night.

The two ASSASSINS *laugh.* BEATRICE *draws the Assassins' hands out from beneath their cloaks. Their fists close tightly. Their arms grow rigid. She walks around them, using the skirts of their cloaks as long bandages and wrapping the two up like mummies, with their clenched fists protruding. She passes her hand over their faces to wipe away their sneering grimaces. After one last look at the* ASSASSINS.

Ah! the weapons!

She goes to LUCRETIA, *who hands her two daggers, which she presses into the Assassins' hands. Returning to the* ASSASSINS.

Go.

She accompanies them out of the room, then re-enters and goes toward LUCRETIA. *A deathly silence falls upon the scene.* BEATRICE *presses both her hands against her heart: she seems about to faint:* LUCRETIA *supports her. Another long pause.*

My God! My God! Quick, I do not think I could endure . . .

A groan can be heard, like the voice of someone talking in his sleep.

LUCRETIA: One would almost think he was speaking.

BEATRICE *shakes her head. The sound of two people running as though in a panic. The two* ASSASSINS *appear, the first dragging after him the other, who hangs back and tries to get loose from his grip. They are both trembling in every limb.*

BEATRICE: Well?

One of the two ASSASSINS *pantomimes the gesture that his courage has failed him. The other that he had tried to do his part but that his partner had dragged him away.*

Cowards! The cowards! they did not dare strike. (*She dashes toward the back of the stage, then returns.*) Where are your weapons?

BEATRICE *runs off stage. A pause. One of the* ASSASSINS

touches the other's arm, indicating LUCRETIA. LUCRE-
TIA *turns toward them and stares hard at them. At
that same moment* BEATRICE *returns.*

The weapons are not in the room—the window is
wide open.

(*To the* ASSASSINS.) You claim to be death-dealers
and yet you are scared of an old man mouthing a
discourse with his conscience in his dreams. Go up
there and split his head in two or *I* shall kill him
with whatever weapon comes to hand and then
accuse you of his death.

The ASSASSINS *go out again, crestfallen. A fairly long
pause. A great cry is heard. The* ASSASSINS *reappear,
bespattered with blood.* BEATRICE *runs off and returns
carrying a bag of money and a sort of ecclesiastical
chasuble glittering with gold, both of which she
thrusts into their hands.*

Go! You have earned your reward.

The ASSASSINS *run off, jostling each other.* CENCI *can
be seen high up, at the back of the stage, staggering,
his fist closed over his right eye as though gripping
some object. At the same time, terrifying fanfares
erupt in ever increasing volume.*

Scene Two

*A drop representing white sky is lowered in front of the
stage setting, and is immediately bathed in a fierce light.
The fanfare recommences, very close and menacing.*

BEATRICE (*clapping her hands over her ears*) : Stop! Stop! The blare of this trumpet stifles me.

LUCRETIA: A fearful sound of doom.

BEATRICE: Surely it is not already the . . . No, no, impossible. All is quiet. All is quiet. I myself hardly realize what has just happened. It is too soon for anyone to have found out.

BERNARDO: Soldiers, soldiers everywhere, Beatrice. I am afraid for you, hide quickly. (*He weeps.*)

BEATRICE: It is too early to be frightened, Bernardo, but too late to weep for what is done.

> BEATRICE *and* BERNARDO *withdraw.* LUCRETIA, *who was moving forward on the side of the stage from where the fanfare was sounding, recoils wildly from a blinding and terrible light that gradually floods the whole stage. The drop is raised without interruption of the action.* BEATRICE, LUCRETIA, BERNARDO *come on stage at the moment when* CAMILLO, *followed by* GUARDS *and preceded by the gleam of a forest of torches, enters from the opposite side.*

LUCRETIA: Camillo!

CAMILLO (*makes a peremptory gesture with his left hand*) : No, not Camillo, but His Holiness' Legate. I must speak to Count Cenci without delay. Is he sleeping?

LUCRETIA: I think he is sleeping!

BEATRICE: He must be sleeping!

CAMILLO: I regret disturbing you, but Count Cenci has to answer charges of the gravest consequence, and at once: that is my mission.

LUCRETIA: No one in our household would dare attempt to wake him.

BEATRICE: No one, truly.

CAMILLO: Then I must wake him myself. Come, quickly, my time is precious.

BERNARDO *has returned stealthily and hides now behind* BEATRICE.

LUCRETIA: Bernardo, conduct the Legate into your father's bedchamber.

CAMILLO, BERNARDO, *two* GUARDS *exit. The others spread themselves out in a semicircle as if trying to surround the two women.* LUCRETIA, *as though walking in her sleep, goes and places herself in the center of this circle.* BEATRICE *stands beside her in a defiant attitude.*

My God! one minute earlier, and Cenci would still be breathing! If only time could move backward!

BEATRICE: I have nothing to weep over. I did what I had to. What is to follow means nothing to me.

LUCRETIA (*listening in despair*): Yes, they are turning the body over . . . They are already suspicious.

Suddenly a great uproar breaks out. Voices cry:

Help! Help! Murder! Murderers . . . there are murderers! . . . after them!

All is lost. It is all up with us.

The uproar dies down as quickly as it started. Silence.

Nothing more. I can hear them guessing the truth.

They are beginning to trace the circle inside which they will imprison us.

A pause. CAMILLO *returns with the* GUARDS.

CAMILLO: Search the whole castle. Guard the doors. From this moment you are all prisoners.

BEATRICE (*running up to him*) : What has happened?

BERNARDO: Beatrice, I am frightened . . . I do not know what to say. Cenci, our father, has been murdered.

BEATRICE: How can that be? I saw him hardly an hour ago. He was sleeping. The weight of his crimes did not seem to be troubling him.

BERNARDO: No, Beatrice, no: murdered. With a nail driven into his head.

BEATRICE *shakes her head.*

LUCRETIA: Murdered! But I alone have the keys of those apartments. No one apart from ourselves could have got in. (*She claps her hand over her mouth, realizing that she has said too much.*)

CAMILLO: Ah! is that so?

He goes up to BERNARDO *and touches him on the shoulder.*

You, answer. If you know anything, speak! Can you suspect who may have murdered him?

BERNARDO: I don't know what to think.

BEATRICE (*interrupting*) : I and my mother, Lucretia, are exhausted: we ask your permission to retire.

The two women move toward the door. CAMILLO
turns toward them and gestures to them to stop.

CAMILLO: One moment. There is too much mystery here.
You shall not leave before telling me . . . Is it true
that your father forced you to submit to outrages so
gross that . . .

BEATRICE: Monsignor, I grant no one the right to pene-
trate my innermost thoughts.

CAMILLO: But in fact, Beatrice, you have desired this death
for a long time . . .

BEATRICE: Monsignor, I beg you, take care: do not be too
eager to jump to false conclusions. (*She shows her
hands, they are spotlessly white. A pause. She motions
with her head, behind her, to indicate the direction
of the room where* CENCI *has met his death.*) The
blood of my father is still fresh.

CAMILLO: There is a secret here, and I am determined to
unravel it.

He makes a sign to the GUARDS, *who immediately surround the two women.* BERNARDO *rushes headlong
inside the circle and throws his arms around* BEATRICE.
CAMILLO *passes through the ring of soldiers and, put-
ting his hand on Bernardo's head, draws him gently
outside the circle with him. The ring of soldiers
re-forms.*

BEATRICE (*with outstretched arms*): For pity's sake! do
not take him away from me.

BERNARDO (*completely hysterical*): No, no, no! Wherever
she goes, I shall follow her.

He hurls himself at the soldiers, beating them with his fists.

LUCRETIA: My God! but it is Cenci himself. Be quiet, Cenci.

BERNARDO: For God's sake kill me. But give me back my soul.

The soldiers thrust him back.

They have sacrificed my soul. They have sacrificed my soul. They have sacrificed my soul . . .

And he repeats these words in a desperate scream as the curtain falls.

Scene Three

From the stage's ceiling, a wheel is revolving on its invisible axis. BEATRICE, *attached to the wheel by her hair, and urged on by a* GUARD *who is gripping her wrists behind her back, follows the direction set by the revolving wheel. Every few steps she takes, screams, accompanied by the sound of turning winches, grinding wheels, or groaning beams, can be heard coming from different directions around the stage. The prison sounds like a busy factory.*

BERNARDO: You hear them . . . The tormenters are at work in every corner of this terrible prison.

BEATRICE: Did you really expect anything but torments from this prison we call life?

BERNARDO, *as though drunk with admiration, moves toward* BEATRICE. *His hands are tied behind his back, but his feet are not chained. He goes in front of her, turning around her, describing a complete circle around her while speaking.*

BERNARDO: Beatrice, I do not know what fate awaits us both, but I can tell you, as I watch you in the act of living, that my own soul could never forget a soul like yours.

A pause. BEATRICE *continues to move in a circle.*

BEATRICE: Goodbye. Cry, but don't despair. For love of yourself be faithful, I beg you, to the love you have pledged me.

The wheel turns. The prison screams.

Do you hear the music? I bequeath you the words to it; they are a sovereign cure for the evils of existence.

Very soft, very sinister music gradually makes itself heard.

Just as a sleeper, lost and groping in a dark dream more fearful than death itself, hesitates before opening his eyes, knowing that to continue in this life means never to wake again—so do I renounce a soul bruised by the harsh business of living, and hurl that soul back in the face of the god who made me, as a blazing fire to cure him of creating.

The soldier has come to a stop, and is weeping. Sounds of commotion from the prison vaults.

BERNARDO: They are coming. Let me kiss your warm lips before the fire which destroys all destroys their smooth petals; before everything which was once Beatrice vanishes like a hurricane.

BEATRICE *puts her arms around him, then looks at him and kisses him, holding him so closely that his body arches backward. Enter* CAMILLO, *with* LUCRETIA, GIACOMO, *and* GUARDS.

CAMILLO *(wiping his face)* : Get this over with, quickly. I feel quite sick with horror.

(To BEATRICE.) Come, confess. Your mute assassins have admitted their guilt in writing.

LUCRETIA: Beatrice, the sin is committed: now we must repent. Why let your limbs be wrenched apart through sheer obstinacy?

GIACOMO: Beatrice, the man who hatched the plot, Orsino, is in flight. He escaped through the Pincian gate disguised as a charcoal seller. There has been enough torture. We are all conspirators and have to pay our debt.

BEATRICE: Pay what debt? I admit the crime, but deny guilt.

CAMILLO: Here is the sentence, and the order for execution. Sign it. And do not hope for pardon.

BEATRICE: The Pope's cruelty matches the cruelty of old Cenci. But I tell you this: it is bad that fathers should band together against the families they have created. I have not had a chance to present my defense before the father of Christianity.

CAMILLO: And your father? Did you give him a chance to present his defense before you crept up to cut his throat?

BERNARDO: She killed in self-defense.

LUCRETIA: Is there a law which commands fathers to devour what they have created and commands sons to let themselves be devoured?

CAMILLO: I am not here to discuss a law of nature, but to bring back to the Pope the signed confession of Beatrice, upon whose crime judgment has already been pronounced.

BERNARDO: By whom?

CAMILLO: By the Pope. He has heard legal pleas on your behalf, but, believe me, though you may have public opinion on your side you will never sway authority.

BEATRICE: They have signed their confessions of guilt. But what heavenly judge could have dared sign mine without blushing with shame at his act?

BERNARDO: There are moments when even the most powerful authority is wise enough to know it must retreat.

LUCRETIA: Hush. The sentences meted out by judges are fearful indeed for those deprived of liberty thereby.

CAMILLO: It is not authority itself that crushes you, but rather the power behind that authority, with which judges weave strange complicities.

He makes BEATRICE *sign the death warrant.*

Untie her. Give them all fresh air, let them go down and prepare themselves for their fate.

(*To* BEATRICE.) Beatrice, may death come to you gently. That is all that is in my power to wish you. I hope that the heavenly judge will be more merciful toward you than was the Pope here on earth.

BEATRICE: Get away from me, Camillo. Let no one ever dare mention the name of God to me again.

BERNARDO: Quick, quick, turn the page; let us try to imagine that none of this ever really happened.

The whole group arranges itself in a sort of pre-execution march, setting off to the sound of an Inca seven-part time rhythm.

BEATRICE: I am going to die, and I tell you that this world has always lived under the sign of injustice. With my death, life itself perishes.

The soldiers, with bowed heads, take up positions at the head of the procession.

CAMILLO (*to* BERNARDO): Your life is spared. You are young, try to forget.

BERNARDO: Live, when the flame which lit my life is about to flicker out!

BEATRICE: Everything dies: the world is burning up, hesitating between good and evil.

A pause.

Neither God nor man, nor any of the forces which dominate what is called our destiny, have chosen between good and evil.

A pause.

I die, and I have not chosen.

The music grows louder. A kind of human voice now mingles its desperate tone with the music's compulsive rhythm.

So young to go away so soon. To be swallowed by the sad, grim earth whose victims curse themselves throughout eternity. The world I leave behind shall not survive me.

LUCRETIA: Man does not destroy the corn in the blade. Man does not burn the newly built town.

BEATRICE: If I die, it is because they have sentenced youth to death.

LUCRETIA: The youth they have destroyed engulfs them in their own tomb.

BEATRICE: I am beautiful, but I have not yet enjoyed my beauty.

LUCRETIA: I am rich, but I have not yet profited from the possessions that a life of deceit seemed to place within my reach. I wash my hands of an abundance that is an insult to poverty.

BEATRICE: My heart, still untouched by enjoyment, must stop before it could ever start beating.

LUCRETIA: Was life, then, molded for this impatient, awful reckoning? I know the injustice of living, but alas! I dare not appeal from it to the justice of dying.

BEATRICE: Oh my eyes, what a dreadful vision you will see, in dying. How can I be sure that, down there, I shall not be confronted by my father? The very notion makes my death more bitter. For I fear that death may teach me that I have ended by resembling him.

The whole procession disappears to the rhythm of the music while the curtain falls very slowly.